AN OUTLINE

OF

THE SYSTEM

OF

EDUCATION

AT

NEW LANARK.

By ROBERT DALE OWEN.

GLASGOW:

Printed at the University Press,

FOR WARDLAW & CUNNINGHAME, GLASGOW;

BELL & BRADFUTE, EDINBURGH; AND

LONGMAN, HURST, REES, ORME, BROWN, & GREEN,

LONDON.

1824.

DEDICATION.

————————

To ROBERT OWEN, Esq.

I DEDICATE this my first production to you, my dear Father, because I trace the formation of a great part of my own character, and the origin of a great part of my own feelings and sentiments to yourself.

In teaching me to think, you led me to examine principles, intimately connected with the best interests of mankind; and I feel that I have derived both pleasure and profit from the examination.

I have seen these principles partially applied to practice, and have witnessed the many beneficial effects which were produced. I have seen their application counteracted by many opposing circumstances, whose influence in rendering the experiment incomplete, had been predicted and explained by the principles themselves.

And it gives me pleasure to know that you are about to commence a more perfect experiment, where practice may uniformly accord with principle; because I believe this to be necessary to prove to the world, that your principles are indeed founded in fact and in true religion.

But its success will scarcely create in my own mind a stronger conviction than I already entertain, of the certainty and facility, with which poverty and vice and misery may be gradually removed from the world.

R. D. OWEN.

INTRODUCTION.

THE system of education which has been introduced at New Lanark, differs essentially from any that has been adopted in a similar institution in the United Kingdom, or, probably, in any other part of the world.

Some particulars regarding it, may, therefore, prove interesting, as exhibiting the results produced on the young mind, by combinations, many of them new, and almost all modified by the general principles on which the system is founded.

It may be necessary to premise, that, the experiment which has been here instituted for the purpose of ascertaining the capabilities of the human mind, at a very early period of life, cannot, by any means, be considered as a full and complete, but, on

the contrary, as merely a partial and imperfect one ; and the results thence obtained,
however satisfactory, not as those which a
system of training, rational and consistent
throughout, may be expected to produce,
but only as a proof—an encouraging one, it
is presumed—of what may be effected even
by a distant approximation to it, under the
counteraction of numerous prejudices and
retarding causes.

The difficulties and disadvantages, inci-
dental to an experiment of this nature, will
be most correctly estimated by those, who
may have had an opportunity of witnessing
the introduction of any new system, however
beneficial ; and the pertinacity with which
old established habits and ideas continue to
hold out against apparently self-evident im-
provements.

Such individuals will give to the following
considerations their due weight :
That, as the children lodge with their
parents, and remain in school during five
hours only, each day, the counteracting
influence of an association with persons who
have not received a similar education, must

be very great, particularly as those persons, whether parents, relations, or elder companions, are such as, from their age and experience, the children generally look up to with respect, and whose habits and manners they are but too apt to adopt implicitly as a model for their own.

That the difficulty was very great in procuring teachers, who, to the requisite fund of knowledge, general and particular, should unite all the various qualifications of habits, and of temper, so essential in a teacher of youth ; unaccompanied too with any pedantry, which might prevent him from regarding his pupils in the light of younger friends, or conversing familiarly with them, and entering into their ideas, or even sometimes into their little projects and amusements, or which might disincline him to be himself, when necessary, instructed and directed.

That, as the parents in general avail themselves of the permission which is granted them, to send their children into the manufactory at ten years of age, the education of these children, being thus broken off at the most interesting and important period, generally remains incomplete; for, although the schools are open in the evening for the instruction of those older children who are employed in the works, yet many do not attend regularly, and it is found that those who do, cannot, after ten hours and a half of labour, apply in the same manner, or derive, by any means, the same benefit from that instruction, as the day scholars.

That many of the children, previously to their admission into the schools, had been permitted to acquire bad habits and improper dispositions, an acquisition which is frequently made, to a great extent, before the little creatures have reached the age of two years, and which most parents, under existing circumstances, have neither the knowledge, nor the means, to prevent. And lastly,

That several of the arrangements, necessary to the completion of the system, are yet only in progress, and that many more remain to be introduced.

NEW LANARK, }
Oct. 1823. }

AN OUTLINE,

&c.

I⊤ will be proper, before proceeding to details, to state the general principles by which these schools are regulated.

The children are governed, not by severity, but by kindness; and excited, not by distinctions, but by creating in them a wish to learn what they are to be taught.

All rewards and punishments whatever, except such as Nature herself has provided, and which it is fortunately impossible, under any system, to do away with, are sedulously excluded, as being equally unjust in themselves, and prejudicial in their effects.

Unjust—as, on the one hand loading those individuals with supposed advantages and distinctions, whom Providence, either in the formation of their talents and dispositions, or in the character of their parents and associates, seems already to have favoured; and on the other, as inflicting farther pain on those, whom less fortunate, or less favourable circumstances, have already formed into weak, vicious, or ignorant,—or in other words, into unhappy beings.

And prejudicial—in rendering a strong, bold character, either proud and overbearing, or vindictive and deceitful; or in instilling into the young mind, if more timid and less decided, either an overweening opinion of its own abilities and endowments, or a dispiriting idea of its own incompetency—such an idea as creates a sullen, hopeless despondency, and destroys that elasticity of spirit, from whence many of our best actions proceed, but which is lost as soon as the individual feels himself sunk, mentally or morally, below his companions, disgraced by punishment, and treated with neglect or contempt by those around him.

It may be a question, which of these two motives, reward or punishment, is in its ultimate effects upon the human character, the more prejudicial, and produces the greater unhappiness; the one in generating pride, vanity, inordinate ambition, and all their concomitant irrational and injurious feelings and passions, or the other in debasing the character, and destroying the energies of the individual. And, in this view, the advocates for such a system might perhaps with some plausibility support its *justice*, by arguing—"that the apparent advantages and distinctions, bestowed on already favoured individuals, often cause them more unhappiness and dissatisfaction, than all the mortifications and disappointments of their seemingly less fortunate companions; and thus tend to equalize the amount of positive advantages acquired by each." But surely such an argument is but a poor defence of the system. It is only supporting its justice at the expense of its expediency.

We have said, that all rewards and punishments were excluded from these schools, except those which nature herself has established. By *natural* rewards and punishments, we mean the *necessary consequences*, immediate and remote, which result from any action.

If happiness be "our being's end and aim," and if that which promotes the great end of our being be right, and that which has a contrary tendency be wrong,—then have we obtained a simple and intelligible definition of right and wrong. It is this: "*Whatever, in its ultimate consequences, increases the happiness of the community, is right; and whatever, on the other hand, tends to diminish that happiness, is wrong.*" A proposition, at once clear in itself, and encouraging in its application; and one which will scarcely be rejected but by those who are unaccustomed to take a comprehensive view of any subject, or whose minds, misled and confused, perhaps, by words without meaning, mistake the *means* for the *end*, and give to those means an importance, which is due to them only in as far as they conduce to the end itself, the great object of all our pursuits, and the secret mainspring of all our actions.

Every action whatever must, on this principle, be followed by its natural reward and punishment; and a clear knowledge and *distinct conviction* of the necessary consequences of any particular line of conduct, is

all that is necessary, however sceptical some
may be on this point, to direct the child in
the way he should go; provided common
justice be done to him in regard to the other
circumstances, which surround him in infancy and childhood. We must carefully
impress on his mind, how intimately connected his *own* happiness is, with that of *the
community*. And the task is by no means
difficult. Nature, after the first impression,
has almost rendered it a sinecure. She will
herself confirm the impression, and fix it in-
delibly on the youthful mind. Her rewards
will confer increasing pleasure, and yet
create neither pride nor envy. Her punishments will prove ever watchful monitors;
but they will neither dispirit nor discourage.
Man is a social being. The pleasures resulting from the exercise of sincerity and of
kindness, of an obliging, generous disposi-
tion, of modesty and of charity, will form,
in his mind, such a striking and ever-present
contrast to the consequences of hypocrisy
and ill-nature, of a disobliging, selfish temper,
and of a proud, intemperate, intolerant
spirit, that he will be induced to consider

the conduct of that individual as little short of insanity, who would hesitate, in any one instance, which course to pursue. He would expect, what appeared to him so self-evident, to be so to every one else ; and feeling himself so irresistibly impelled in the course he followed, and deriving from it, daily and hourly, new gratification, he must be at a loss to conceive, what could have blinded the eyes, and perverted the understanding of one who was pursuing, with the greatest difficulty and danger to himself, an opposite course, pregnant with mortification in its progress, and disappointment in its issue ; employing all his powers to increase his own misery, and throwing from him true, genuine happiness, to grasp for the hundredth time, some momentary gratification, if that deserve the name, which he knew by experience would but leave him more dissatisfied and miserable than it found him.

And his surprise would be very natural, if he were not furnished with the clew, which can alone unravel what appears so palpably inconsistent with the first dictates of human nature. That clew would enable him to trace the origin of such inconsistency to the system of education at present pursued, generally speaking, over the world. Artificial rewards and punishments are introduced; and the child's notions of right and wrong are so confused *by the substitution of these, for the natural consequences resulting from his conduct,*—his mind is, in most cases, so thoroughly imbued with the uncharitable notion, that whatever he has been taught to consider wrong, deserves immediate punishment; and that he himself is treated unjustly, unless rewarded for what he believes to be right;—that it were next to a miracle, if his mind did not become more or less irrational: or if he chose a course, which, otherwise, would have appeared too self-evidently beneficial to be rejected.

The principles that regulate the instruction at New Lanark, preclude any such ideas. A child who acts improperly, is not considered an object of *blame*, but of *pity*. His instructors are aware, that a practical knowledge of the effects of his conduct is all that is required, in order to induce him to change it. And this knowledge they endeavour to give him. They show him the intimate, inseparable, and immediate connection of his own happiness, with that of those around him; a principle which, to an unbiased mind, requires only a fair statement to make it evident; and the practical observance of which, confers too much pleasure to be abandoned for a less generous or more selfish course.

In cases where admonition is necessary, it is given in the spirit of kindness and of charity, as from the more experienced, to the less experienced. The former, having been taught wherein true self-interest consists, are aware, that had the individual who has just been acting improperly, had the knowledge and the power given him, to form his character, he would, *to a certainty*, have excluded from its composition such feelings, as those in which his offence originated; because that knowledge would have informed him, that these were only calculated to diminish his own happiness. The presence of those feelings would constitute the surest proof, that the knowledge and the power had been denied him.

Such, at least, would be the inference we should deduce from similar conduct, in any parallel case. Let us suppose a traveller anxious to reach the end of his journey. He is young and inexperienced, and perfectly unacquainted with the country through which he is to pass. Two roads are before him: the one is smooth and pleasant, affording, at every turn, some new and animating prospect; it leads directly to his object; if he follow it, he will every where meet with agreeable and intelligent companions, all travelling in the same direction, and all anxious to give him every information and assistance. The other, though at first not uninviting, soon becomes dangerous and rugged, leading through a bleak, waste country, the prospect on every side dismal and discouraging; he who pursues it will be continually beset by thieves and assassins; he must be prepared, in every individual he meets, to discover a rival or an enemy; all his fellow-travellers will conceive it to be their interest to mislead and perplex him; for they know that the inns are few, and small and ill supplied, and that every

additional companion lessens the chance of
adequate accommodation for themselves :
this road, too, dangerous and difficult and
disagreeable as it is, gradually changes its
direction ; it will lead the unfortunate traveller, if indeed he survive its perils and hard-
ships, farther and farther from the object of
his destination, and will at last probably
conduct him into a strange, barbarous country, where he will sit down in despair, fa-
tigued and harassed, dissatisfied with himself, displeased with his fellow-creatures, dis-
gusted with his journey, and equally afraid
and unwilling either to proceed, or to return.

Our traveller, however, chooses this latter
path in preference to the other. Now, can
we suppose it a possible case, that, at the
time he did so, he knew what he was choosing. It is admitted that he *had* a choice,
and that he chose evil, and rejected good.
But should we therefore assume that he *himself created the preference which gave rise to
that choice* ; that he *wilfully formed an erroneous judgment* ; and that he merited pain and
punishment by such perversity ? Should we

not rather conclude, either that he had decided at random, unconscious of the importance of his choice, or had been deceived by a casual review of the general appearance of the country? Could we avoid remarking, that circumstances which he had not created, and which he could neither alter nor regulate, induced a preference, and thus determined his choice? And if we attempted to put him into the right path, would our language be that of anger or violence? Should we consider it necessary to employ any *artificial* inducements in urging him to change his course? or should we not rather conclude, that this would only lead him to suspect our disinterestedness, and confirm him in the resolution he had already adopted? Nay, if, to ensure his safety and comfort, we proceeded to actual force, and obliged him to take the other path, is it not but too probable, that, as soon as he was relieved of our troublesome presence, he would strike into the first cross-road that presented itself, to return to his original course? How much more easily would the proposed end be effected by a simple dispassionate statement of facts, unaccompanied by violence, and unattended by any artificial inducement! How much more wise would be our conduct if we endeavoured to procure a map of the country, and to prove to the traveller the accuracy of the information we gave; or if we advised him to enquire of those who might be returning from the road he had been so anxious to follow, whether *they* had found it a pleasant or a direct one. They would at once tell him the real state of the case. We might then endeavour to induce him to accompany us in the other direction, only requiring of him that he should look, and hear, and judge for himself.

Now, I believe it to be impossible, that, with even a moderate knowledge of human nature, we should not be able to prove to this traveller, young and inexperienced, and uninformed as he is, our sincerity in the advice we had given him; and I am equally certain, that if we did so, and he believed our statement, he *could* not *deliberately make himself miserable, in preference to making himself happy;* otherwise the desire of happiness cannot be a universal law of our nature.

In the case just stated, the traveller is supposed to commence his journey alone. If he were accompanied by many companions of his own age, and if they all struck into the opposite road, we admit it to be possible that advice and even conviction might be inefficient to prevent him from going along with them. Man is gregarious; and he might choose to traverse a desert in the company of others, though it led to danger and to death, in preference to beginning a *solitary* journey, though it conducted through gardens to a paradise. But, on the other hand, if his companions followed the road to happiness, it would scarcely be necessary to warn *him* of the danger of separating from them and choosing the other path. If, indeed, *example* and *advice* proved equally unavailing in inducing him to accept of happiness, then nothing less than insanity would account for his conduct; and even in such a case, violence or artificial inducements would prove ineffectual.

We might safely build on a rock, and yet we prefer a bank of sand, artificially supported on all sides, with infinite trouble and

anxiety and expense, and which, in all likeli-
hood, the first flood will carry along with it!

Let us suppose a set of children, overawed
by the fear of punishment, and stimulated
by the hope of reward, kept, which is but
seldom the case, during the presence of their
teachers in what is called " trim order," apparently all diligence and submission; will
these children, we ask, when the teacher's
back is turned, and this artificial stimulus
ceases to operate, continue to exhibit the
same appearance? or are they not much
more likely to glory in an opportunity of
running into the opposite extreme, and
thereby exonerating themselves of a restraint so irksome? Nay, more : impressed
as they are with the idea that pleasure and
duty run counter to each other, and that,
therefore, rewards and punishments are employed to induce them to follow duty at the
expense of pleasure, can we expect that such
individuals should in after life hesitate to
reap present gratification from any line of
conduct, not immediately followed by artificial punishment? for that is a *criterion of
right and wrong*, which had been brought

home to their feelings in too forcible a manner to be quickly forgotten, or easily effaced. Can we wonder that so few individuals leave our schools with other impressions than these? If we do, we surely forget that the law of cause and effect applies equally in the formation of the human character, as in that of a blade of grass or any other natural production.

It is scarcely necessary to allude to the difference which will be found in the character of those, who have never felt these artificial excitements, and whose *youthful* actions have been regulated by a principle, which will operate equally *in after life*. *They* will know that virtue always conducts to happiness, and that vice leads only to misery; and therefore, they will follow virtue from its own excellence, and avoid vice from its own deformity.

Obstinacy and wilfulness are often fostered, even in generous minds, by a feeling of independence, in rejecting what is attempted to be forced upon them. And public opinion confirms this feeling. He obtains, among his school-fellows, the character of a brave, spirited fellow, who will set himself—whether right or wrong—against the will of their mutual tyrant, for that is the light in which they are too often obliged to regard their instructors. In an institution, conducted on correct principles, the scene is reversed. No credit is obtained, where no risk is incurred. Public opinion is against those who refuse obedience to, or elude commands, which, it is known, are never given but on a reasonable occasion, or enforced, but in a mild and gentle manner. *Obedience* is never confounded with *cowardice*, and therefore obedience is popular. The most generous and intelligent individuals uniformly lead their companions, and these are gained, when they see themselves treated in a generous and intelligent manner. No party is formed against the authority of the teachers; for even a schoolboy's generosity will not oppose force to mildness, or determined obstinacy to uniform kindness. The teachers are loved, not feared, yet without any deduction from their authority, whenever they find it necessary to exert it. Their pupils converse with them out of school hours, or even during the lessons, when it can be done with propriety, with the most perfect ease and freedom, and such conversation is regarded as a privilege. In the New Lanark institution, this practice has already led to questions and remarks from the children themselves, which would be considered far above their years, and than which nothing can be a greater proof of the good effects of this system of instruction.

What the children have to learn, is conveyed to them in as pleasant and agreeable a manner as can be devised. The subject is selected, and treated with a view to interest them as much as possible. In the lectures, to which we shall presently have occasion to allude, if the interest or attention is observed to flag, the teacher looks to *the lecture itself*, and to his *manner of delivering it*, rather than *to the children*, to discover the cause. It is on this principle, that sensible signs and conversation are made the medium of instruction, whenever it is practicable; and this plan, dictated by nature, has been found to be eminently useful.

Their attention is never confined too long

to one object : a lesson for the day scholars, in any particular branch, never exceeding three quarters of an hour.

No unnecessary restraint is imposed on the children ; but, on the contrary, every liberty is allowed them, consistently with good order, and attention to the exercise in which they may be engaged.

By a steady adherence to such a system, but little difficulty will be experienced, in mildly enforcing whatever has once been required of the scholars ; even in cases where they may perceive neither the immediate nor ultimate benefit of a compliance.

These principles are no plausible, unsupported theory. Even as such, they appear conclusive. In the absence of any direct experiment, their consistency with every thing we see around us, and with the first feelings and dictates of our nature, would give them no inconsiderable weight. But an experiment has been made under every disadvantage,—what has been done in school has been counteracted without,—(for most of the parents, as was to be expected, do not yet comprehend the utility of this mode of instruction, and have continued their system of rewards and punishments); the teachers themselves have discovered the practice of the system but by degrees; it has been attacked and denounced even by those who had been connected with it—has been cramped by imperfect arrangements; and checked by a mixture of the old with the new principles and practices, inseparable from a first trial;—and yet the result, much as it falls short of what, under different circumstances, might have been obtained, has been, in a very high degree, satisfactory. No such result, as far as we are aware, has hitherto been produced in any similar institution; it is a result, too, which is obtained in the most agreeable manner, both for the instructors and the instructed, without repressing a single generous feeling, and without incurring the risk of abandoning the schoolboy to the world, either as a determined violator of law and of principle, or as a mean, undecided, dispirited character, equally afraid to do wrong, and unwilling to do right.

Having thus adverted to the general principles by which these schools are governed, the full discussion of which might easily be extended to volumes, and is consequently foreign to our present purpose, we proceed to lay before the public an outline of the details of the plan.

———————

The "New Institution," or School, which is open for the instruction of the children and young people connected with the establishment, to the number of about 600*, consists of two stories. The upper story, which is furnished with a double range of windows, one above the other, all round, is divided into two apartments; one, which is the principal school-room, fitted up with desks and forms, on the Lancasterian plan, having a free passage down the centre of the room, is about 90 feet long, 40 feet broad, and 20 feet high. It is surrounded, except

* Of these about 300 are day scholars, under ten years of age. The rest are above that age, and attend in the evening when their work is completed; in summer, however, their number is considerably below that here stated.

at one end, where a pulpit stands, with galleries, which are convenient, when this room is used, as it frequently is, either as a lecture room or place of worship.

The other apartment, on the second floor, is of the same width and height as that just mentioned, but only 49 feet long. The walls are hung round with representations of the most striking zoological and mineralogical specimens; including quadrupeds, birds, fishes, reptiles, insects, shells, minerals, &c. At one end there is a gallery, adapted for the purpose of an orchestra, and at the other are hung very large representations of the two hemispheres; each separate country, as well as the various seas, islands, &c. being differently coloured, but without any names attached to them. This room is used as a lecture and ball-room, and it is here, that the dancing and singing lessons are daily given. It is likewise occasionally used as a reading room for some of the classes.

The lower story is divided into three apartments, of nearly equal dimensions, 12 feet high, and supported by hollow iron pillars, serving, at the same time, as conductors, in winter, for heated air, which issues through the floor of the upper story, and by which means the whole building may, with ease, be kept at any required temperature. It is in these three apartments that the younger classes are taught reading, natural history, and geography.

We may here remark, that it is probable, the facility of teaching the older classes particularly, would have been greatly increased, had some part of the building been divided into smaller apartments, appropriating one to each class of from twenty to thirty children, provided such an arrangement had not encroached either on the lecture room, or principal school-room.

Each of the two elder classes for the boys, and the same for the girls, who at that age are taught reading, writing, &c. separately from the boys, and only meet them during the lectures, and in the lessons in singing and dancing, consists of from twenty to forty children. The younger classes, composed indiscriminately of boys and girls, are rather more numerous. A master is appointed to each class. There are likewise, attached to the institution, a master who teaches dancing and singing, a drilling master, and a sewing mistress.

At present the older classes are taught reading, writing, &c. in different parts of the principal school-room, the size of which prevents any confusion from such an arrangement; but, as was before observed, the facility with which their attention could be gained, would probably be greatly increased, could a separate apartment be appropriated to each class. The very size of the room, too, increases the difficulty, of itself no slight one, of modulating the voice in reading.

The hours of attendance, in the day school, are from half past seven till nine, from ten till twelve, and from three till five in the afternoon. In winter, however, instead of coming to school again in the afternoon from three to five, the children remain, with an interval of half an hour, from ten till two o'clock, when they are dismissed for the day; making the same number of hours in summer and in winter.

The ages of the children are from eighteen months to ten or sometimes twelve years.

They are allowed to remain at school as long as their parents will consent to their doing so; though the latter generally avail themselves of the permission which is granted them, to send their children into the manufactory at ten years of age, or soon after. It is the wish of the founder of these schools, that the parents should not require their children to attend a stated employment till they are at least twelve years old; and it cannot admit of a doubt, that the general adoption of such a measure would be productive of the most important advantages to the-parents themselves, to the children, and to society at large.

The infant classes, from two to five years, remain in school only one half of the time mentioned as the regular hours of attendance for the other classes. During the remainder of the time, they are allowed to amuse themselves at perfect freedom, in a large paved area in front of the Institution, under the charge of a young woman, who finds less difficulty—and without harshness or punishment—in taking charge of, and rendering contented and happy, one hundred of these little creatures, than most individuals, in a similar situation, experience in conducting a nursery of two or three children. By this means, these infants acquire healthful and hardy habits; and are, at the same time, trained to associate in a kind and friendly manner with their little companions; thus practically learning the pleasure to be derived from such conduct, in opposition to envious bickerings, or ill-natured disputes.

The school is open in the evening to the children and young persons, from 10 to 20 years of age; the system pursued with them is so similar to that adopted in the day school, that in describing the one, we shall give an accurate idea of the other also.

The dress worn by the children in the day school, both boys and girls, is composed of strong white cotton cloth, of the best quality that can be procured. It is formed in the shape of the Roman tunic, and reaches, in the boys dresses, to the knee, and in those of the girls, to the ancle. These dresses are changed three times a week, that they may be kept perfectly clean and neat.

The parents of the older children pay 3d. a month for their instruction. Nothing is paid for the infant classes, or for the evening scholars. This charge is intended merely to prevent them from regarding the Institution with the feelings connected with a charity school. It does not amount to one-twentieth part of the expenses of the school, which is supported by the proprietors of the establishment.

It has been deemed necessary, in order to meet the wishes of the parents, to commence teaching the children the elements of reading, at a very early age; but it is intended that this mode should, ultimately, be superseded, at least until the age of seven or eight, by a regular course of natural history, geography, ancient and modern history, chemistry, astronomy, &c. on the principle, that it is following the plan prescribed by nature, to give a child such particulars as he can easily be made to understand, concerning the *nature and properties* of the different objects around him, before we proceed to teach him the *artificial signs* which have been adopted to represent these objects. It is equally impolitic and irrational, at once to disgust him by a method to him obscure or unintelligible, and consequently tedious and uninteresting, of obtaining that knowledge, which may, in the meantime, be agreeably communicated by conversation, and illustrated by sensible signs; and which may thus, by giving the child a taste for learning, render the attainments of reading and writing really interesting to him, as the means of conferring increased facilities, in acquiring further information.

The following are the branches of instruction at present taught at New Lanark.

READING.

Great difficulty has been experienced, in procuring proper school books for the different classes. Those at present in use, are in many respects defective: they are but ill adapted to the capacities of children so young, and are consequently not calculated to interest them sufficiently. An exception to this last observation must however be made in favour of Miss Edgeworth's little works; but even these contain too much of praise and blame, to admit of their being regarded as unexceptionable. From some little volumes of voyages and travels, too, illustrated by plates and maps, and interspersed with amusing and characteristic anecdotes, great assistance has been derived. The elder classes have often only one copy of each work, from which one of their number reads aloud to the others, who are generally questioned, after a few sentences have been read, as to the substance of what they have just heard. In their answers, they are not confined to the author's words; on the contrary, their answering in a familiar manner, and employing such expressions, as they themselves best understand, is considered as a proof, that they have attended more to the sense, than to the sound.

The general principle, that children should never be directed to read what they cannot understand, has been found to be of the greatest use. The invaluable habit of endeavouring to understand what is read or heard is thus formed. That great and general error, the mistaking of the *means* for the *end*, is avoided, and the erroneous idea excluded, that acquiring a knowledge of the *medium,* through which instruction may be conveyed, is the acquisition of the instruction itself. The children, therefore, after having become acquainted with that medium, will not rest satisfied with this mere mechanical attainment. A knowledge of reading and writing is considered but as furnishing a child with tools, which may be employed for the most useful, or most pernicious purposes, or which may be rusty and unemployed in the possession of him, who having obtained them at great trouble and expense, is yet unacquainted with their real use. The listlessness and indifference so generally complained of by him, whose unpleasant duty it becomes, to force learned, but to them unmeaning sounds, upon his ill-fated pupils, who are thinking of nothing all the time, but the minute that is to free them from the weary task,—are scarcely known under such a system.*

* That the system *actually in practice* at New Lanark is imperfect, and consequently incapable of uniformly producing all the results, which would otherwise be obtained—has already been stated.

It is for this reason, that, but for the wishes of the parents, and of parties connected with the establishment, the Scriptures and Church Catechism would not be put into the hands of children, at so early an age as that of the day scholars. There are many parts of the Scriptures, which children of that age should not be made acquainted with, and many more which they cannot understand; and the Catechism of the Scotch Church is so abstruse and doctrinal, that even their superiors in age and understanding might be puzzled, if called upon to explain, what, as children, they learned to repeat.

The children are taught to read according to the sense, and, as nearly as possible, as they would speak; so as, at once, to show, that they comprehend what they are reading, and to give their companions an opportunity of comprehending it likewise. In order to teach them the proper tone and modulation of the voice, the master frequently reads to his class some interesting work; he then allows his pupils to ask any questions, or make any remarks, that may occur to them.

WRITING.

The mode of teaching writing, is, in the commencement, nearly the same as that adopted in most schools; but as soon as the children can write a tolerably fair text copy, the master begins to teach them current hand writing, according to a plan which has been lately adopted in various seminaries. By this method the children write without lines; and with a little attention, soon learn to correct the stiff formal school hand, generally written, into a fair, legible business hand, such as shall be useful to them in after life.

The writing copies consist of short sentences, generally illustrative of some subject connected with history or geography; and the pupils finally proceed to copy from dictation, or from a book or manuscript, any passage that may be considered as difficult, and at the same time important to be retained in their memory. Thus, as soon as possible, applying the newly acquired medium of instruction in the most efficacious manner.

ARITHMETIC

Has hitherto been taught on the system which commonly prevails in Scotland. The elder classes, however, are just beginning a regular course of mental arithmetic, similar to that adapted by M. Pestalozzi of Iverdun in Switzerland. In this, as in every other department of instruction, the pupils are taught to *understand* what they are doing; the teacher explains to them *why* the different operations, if performed as directed, must be correct; and in what way the knowledge they are acquiring, may be beneficially employed in after life.

SEWING.

All the girls, except those in the two youngest classes, are taught sewing, including knitting, marking, cutting out, &c. One day of the week is appointed, when they are desired to bring to school any of their garments (which must previously have been

washed) that may require mending, and
these they are taught to repair as neatly as
possible.

NATURAL HISTORY, GEOGRAPHY, AND ANCIENT AND MODERN HISTORY.

These studies are classed together, because, though distinct in themselves, and
embracing, each of them, so great a fund of
information, they are taught at New Lanark
nearly in the same manner; that is to say,
in familiar lectures, delivered extempore, by
the teachers. These lectures are given in
classes of from 40 to 50. The children are
subsequently examined regarding what they
have heard; by which means the teacher
has an opportunity of ascertaining, whether
each individual pupil be in possession of the
most important part of the lecture which he
has attended. In these lectures, material
assistance is derived from the use of sensible
signs, adapted to the subject, and which we
shall explain more particularly in their place.
Each master selects a particular branch, and
delivers, as has been already stated, a short
lecture to 40 or 50 children at once. The

number was formerly from 120 to 150 in one class; but this was found much too large, and one half or one third of that number is as many as it is found expedient to assemble together, except when the lecture is so interesting, as at once to rivet every child's attention, and so easily understood, as to require no subsequent explanation whatever. The attainment of this very important point, it may be observed, will require great attention, considerable ability, and a correct knowledge of human nature. It is extremely difficult for the teacher, particularly if he has had but little experience in delivering lectures to children, to preserve the proper medium between too much and too little detail—to distinguish between unnecessary particulars, which will only divert the attention from the main subject, and those, which are absolutely necessary to children, in the way of explanation. By the former, we refer to such particulars as relate to abstruse questions, to politics, to uninteresting, tedious descriptions of particular animals or countries, especially if these differ but slightly from each other; to any thing, in short, that is not striking and interesting in itself, or becomes so, as illustrative of some general principle, or characteristic of some leading feature. To the latter will belong such simple and distinct details, as may explain the phenomena of nature, of science, or of civilization, together with such as tend to create enlarged ideas, to repress illiberal or uncharitable sentiments on any subject, or to teach children to value every thing for its real worth, and prevent their being misled by the relation of events, which are too often held up as glorious and praiseworthy, but which, reason teaches us, are equally irrational and injurious to the happiness of the community.

In commencing the exposition of any subject, too great pains cannot be taken to avoid all minor details, and, first of all, to give the pupils a distinct outline of what is to be taught them ; and to impress this so clearly and definitely on their minds, that they shall be enabled to arrange any subsequent details accordingly. This outline should then be only partially filled up, selecting the most important features, and illustrating these by characteristic anecdotes at greater or less length; than which nothing impresses more distinctly or durably on the mind of a child, the subject to which such anecdote may relate. Subsequently, when further advanced, the pupils may be safely allowed, without fear of perplexing, or overloading their minds, to enter into any important details; and these they will be able at once to classify and appreciate.*

These are the general principles, which regulate the instruction which is given on such subjects, at New Lanark. We are aware how difficult it frequently proves, to deduce from general principles, their practical application; but this difficulty, in the present case, experience will gradually remove.

Natural History is taught to all the scholars, even to the youngest, or infant classes; who can understand and become interested in a few simple particulars regarding such domestic animals as come under their own observation, if these are communicated in a sufficiently familiar manner; for this, in-

---

* As a specimen of the manner in which such an outline is communicated to the scholars, see Appendix.

deed, is almost the first knowledge which Nature directs an infant to acquire.

In commencing a course of Natural History, the division of Nature into the Animal, Vegetable, and Mineral Kingdoms, is first explained to them, and in a very short time they learn at once to distinguish to which of these any object which may be presented to them, belongs.* The teacher then proceeds to details of the most interesting objects furnished by each of these kingdoms, including descriptions of quadrupeds, birds, fishes, reptiles, and insects—and of the most interesting botanical and mineralogical specimens. These details are illustrated by representations of the objects, drawn on a large scale, and as correctly as possible. It is desirable, that these representations should be all on the

---

* Even in the course of such simple illustrations, considerable powers of mind may be elicited. In one of the younger classes at New Lanark, to which the teacher had been explaining this division, the pupils were asked to which kingdom the plaster with which the ceiling of the room was covered, belonged. They answered, "To the Mineral Kingdom;" but one little fellow added, "and to the Animal Kingdom too." And on being asked why? he replied, "Because there is hair in it, and that once belonged to an animal."

same scale ; otherwise the child's idea of their
relative size becomes incorrect. These drawings may be either hung round the room, or
painted, as the botanical representations at
New Lanark are, on glazed canvass, which is
rolled from one cylinder to another, both cylinders being fixed on an upright frame, at
about six or eight feet distance from each
other, so as to show only that length of canvass at once. These cylinders are turned by
means of a handle, which may be applied to
the one, or to the other, as the canvass is to
be rolled up or down.

The classes are subsequently, individually,
encouraged to repeat what they have heard,
to express their opinions on it freely, and to
ask any explanation. Such examinations enable the teacher to ascertain, what parts of
the lecture have been most suited to the capacities, or calculated to call forth the attention, of the children ; and, on the contrary,
what portions were too abstruse and uninteresting to be retained. He is thus daily directed
in his choice of materials for future lectures ;
and he gradually discovers the extent of the
powers of mind which his pupils possess.

In commencing a course of Geography, the children are taught the form of the earth, its general divisions into Land and Water, the subdivisions of the land into four Continents, and into larger and smaller Islands, that of the water into Oceans, Seas, Lakes, &c.; then the names of the principal countries, and of their capitals, together with the most striking particulars concerning their external appearance, natural curiosities, manners and customs, &c. &c. The different countries are compared with our own, and with each other.

The minds of the children are thus opened, and they are prevented from contracting narrow, exclusive notions, which might lead them to regard those only as proper objects of sympathy and interest, who may live in the same country with themselves—or to consider that alone as right, which they have been accustomed to see—or to suppose those habits and those opinions to be the standard of truth and of perfection, which the circumstances of their birth and education have rendered their own. In this manner are the circumstances, which induce national peculiarities and national vices, exhibited to them; and the question will naturally arise in their minds: "Is it not highly probable that we ourselves, had we lived in such a country, should have escaped neither its peculiarities, nor its vices—that we should have adopted the notions and prejudices there prevalent? in fact is it not evident, that we might have been Cannibals or Hindoos, just as the circumstance of our birth should have placed us, in Hindoostan, where the killing of an animal becomes a heinous crime; or amongst some savage tribe, where to torture a fellow creature, and to feast on his dead body, is accounted a glorious action?" A child who has once felt what the true answer to such a question must be, cannot remain uncharitable or intolerant.

The children acquire a knowledge of the zones, and other artificial divisions of the earth; and it is explained to them, that these are not actual and necessary, but merely imaginary and arbitrary divisions, and that they might have been very different, without in any way altering the real and natural divisions of our globe.

Any one of the older classes at New Lanark, on being told the latitude and longitude
of a place, can at once point it out; can say
in what zone it is situated, and whether
therefore, from its situation, it is a hot or a
cold country—what is the number of degrees
of latitude and longitude between it, and any
other given country, even though on the opposite hemisphere; together, probably, with
other details regarding the country; as for
instance, whether it is fertile, or a desert;
what is the colour and general character, and
what the religion of its inhabitants; what
animals are found there; when, and by whom
it was discovered; what is the shortest way
from England to that country; what is the
name of the capital city, and of the principal
mountains and rivers; and perhaps relate
something of its history, or a variety of characteristic anecdotes which he may have heard
regarding it. They can thus travel, as it
were, over the whole world, taking all the
principal countries in rotation.

In the course of the lectures, numerous
opportunities present themselves to commu-
nicate much general information, not strictly

connected with the branches themselves ; as
for example, descriptions of natural phenomena, of trades, manufactures, &c. Thus,
in short, furnishing them with whatever is
useful or pleasant, or interesting for them to
know.

Ancient and Modern History constitutes
another branch of their education. It may
be thought, that in teaching History, the aid
of sensible signs can be but seldom called in.
The reverse, however, is the case. Their
application here is, in fact, more complete
than in any other branch. Seven large maps
or tables, laid out on the principle of the
Stream of Time, and which were originally
purchased from Miss Whitwell, a lady who
formerly conducted a respectable seminary
in London—are hung round a spacious room.
These, being made of canvass, may be rolled
up at pleasure. On the Streams, each of
which is differently coloured, and represents
a nation, are painted the principal events
which occur in the history of those nations.
Each century is closed by a horizontal line,
drawn across the map. By means of these
maps, the children are taught the outlines of

Ancient and Modern History, with ease to
themselves, and without being liable to con-
found different events, or different nations.
On hearing of any two events, for instance,
the child has but to recollect the situation,
on the tables, of the paintings, by which these
are represented, in order to be furnished at
once with their chronological relation to each
other. If the events are cotemporary, he
will instantly perceive it. When the formation and subdivisions of large empires are
represented, the eye seizes the whole at once ;
for wherever the coloured stream of one nation extends over another, on these tables, it
is indicative, either of the subjection of one
of them, or of their union ; and their subsequent separation would be expressed by the
two streams diverging again. The children
can therefore point out the different historical
events, as they do the countries on the map of
the world, count the years and centuries as
they do the degrees of latitude and longitude ;
and acquire an idea almost as clear and tangi-
ble of the history of the world, as that which
the first terrestrial globe they may have seen,
gave them of its form and divisions. We

know, ourselves, how easily we can call to mind any events, representations of which we were, as children, accustomed to see, and we may thence estimate the tenacity with which such early impressions are retained.

The intimate connexion between Natural History, Geography, and History, is evident, so that in lecturing on one of these subjects, the teacher finds many opportunities of recalling to the minds of his pupils various portions of the others.

RELIGION.

The founder of the schools at New Lanark has been accused of bringing up the children without religion.

The direct and obvious tendency of the whole system of education there, most fully warrants, as it appears to us, a representation the very reverse of this; and as much has been asserted, and still more insinuated on the subject, we may be allowed to state our reasons for this opinion.

An acquaintance with the works of the Deity, such as these children acquire, must lay the basis of true religion. The uniform consistency of such evidence, all nations, and all sects, at once acknowledge. No diversity of opinion can exist with regard to it. It is an evidence with which every one who is really anxious that his children should adopt a true religion, must wish them to become acquainted; whether he may have been born in a Christian country, or be a disciple of Mahomet, or a follower of Bramah. Because simple facts can never mislead, or prejudice the mind. They can never support a religion which is false; they must always support one which is true. He who hesitates to receive them as the basis of his religion, tacitly acknowledges its inconsistency. "And where there is inconsistency, there is error." If the subsequent religious instruction, which a child is to receive, be true, then will the instructor derive, in teaching it, the greatest assistance from the store of natural facts, which the child has previously acquired; because true religion must be completely in unison with all facts. If such subsequent instruction be false, then will it certainly become a difficult task to induce a belief in its truth, because a child, whose mind has been thus prepared, will probably soon discover, that it is not in accordance with what he knows to be true; but every one must admit the advantage of such a difficulty. Even supposing a child instructed in true religion, and believing it implicitly, without, however, having acquired that belief by deducing its truth from known or well accredited facts,—upon what foundation can such a belief be said to rest? The first sceptic he may converse with, will probably excite a doubt of its truth in his mind; and he himself, being unable to defend his opinions, and having no means of reasoning on the subject, may soon become a violent opposer of that religion, which, though true, had yet been taught to him before he had acquired sufficient knowledge to understand its evidence, or was capable of judging of its truth or falsehood.

This reasoning is peculiarly applicable in the case of any religion, the evidence for which is chiefly derived from historical deductions.

In any other study, the inconsistency of expecting the pupils to deduce correct conclusions before the facts upon which the reasoning proceeds, are known to them, would be glaringly evident. Why then lose sight of this consideration upon a subject so important as religion?

If a chemist were anxious that a child should be able to trace and understand some valuable and important deductions, which with great study and much patient investigation, he had derived from certain chemical facts; would he act wisely in insisting that the child should at once commit to memory, and implicitly believe these deductions? Would he act consistently in objecting to a system, which should first teach the pupil the elements of chemistry, should gradually store his mind with chemical facts, and at length, when his judgment had become matured, place before him these important deductions, and allow him to judge for himself, as to their accuracy?

What should we think of a professor of chemistry, who should object to such a plan? Who would join with him in stigmatizing, as an infidel in the great principles of chemistry, or in denouncing as an enemy to the science itself, the man who expressed his conviction, that it was irrational, before the child could know any thing of the *elementary principles* of the science, to insist upon its *ultimate deductions?* Would not the chemist, who expressed a fear, that unless these were received and implicitly believed *in infancy,* they would not be received or believed *at all,* excite, by the expression of such an opinion, a suspicion of their truth or accuracy?

And is religion a less important, or a less abstruse science than chemistry? Is it of minor consequence that no such cause should exist for attaching suspicion to the great truths of religion? Or are religious doctrines more easily understood than chemical deductions? Or are they not, perhaps, like these, founded on facts? If they are not, they stand not on a rock, but on a sandy foundation. If they are—as it is presumed they must be—then is a knowledge of these facts a necessary preliminary to the study of the science of religion.

As such, it is communicated to the children in the schools at New Lanark.

And on this principle it is considered, that a child, at an early age, should become acquainted with facts, instead of being instructed in abstruse doctrinal points. If it often requires all the powers of the most matured human reason to decide on these points, surely we do wrong to present any of them to the minds of children. Such a proceeding only serves to puzzle and perplex them: it creates listless and inattentive habits: in most cases, it gives children a decided dislike to the study itself. They learn to regard religion, and every thing connected with it, as gloomy, tiresome and mystical; fit only for those, who have lost all power or opportunity of enjoying any thing else.

It would be a libel on religion to suppose these to be the natural consequences of teaching it to children. They are only the necessary results of forcing on the young mind, the prevalent ideas on this subject. Under a different system a religion of confidence, and peace, and love, and charity, could produce neither fear, nor disgust; nor could it ever become unattractive, if presented to

E

children in a simple and natural light. But, in teaching it, we must not depart from those principles, which regulate the rest of our instruction. We must not expect, that children should like a study, which does not interest them, or should feel interested in a study, which they do not understand. If we do, we shall infallibly meet with the results, which alone, as experience tells us, such a system is calculated to produce. But let us not designate these, either the natural consequences of teaching religion, or evidences of the original corruption of the human heart.

If we plant a healthy vine-shoot in an excellent soil; but if, at the same time, being unacquainted with the proper mode of cultivating vines, we neglect to water it, and surround it with a variety of shrubs, by way of support, which, instead of answering this purpose, cramp the growth of the plant, exclude the sun from it, and render it weak and barren; let us not be surprised at the unhappy results of our management; or conclude that no vines planted in that ground can ever flourish or bear valuable fruit; neither let us libel the soil, by imputing to it original, irremediable barrenness. Let us rather inquire if our treatment of the plant be such as nature dictates, or as, reasoning from analogy, and from our previous knowledge of agriculture, we are warranted in supposing conducive to its successful culture. Otherwise it should cease to be matter of surprise, if we find vines flourishing luxuriantly even in wild, neglected spots, while, under our care, they go to decay, and become but a nuisance and a vexation.

To speak without a metaphor—it is not only a fact, that true religion requires no artificial supports, but it is likewise certain, that by surrounding it with these, we only exclude the light of reason, and render principles suspected, the truth of which, if they had not been thus hidden, and obscured, would long since have established itself on the most solid basis.

Again—we are told, that the heart of man "is deceitful above all things, and desperately wicked." And it is undeniable, that the present character of mankind is neither a sincere nor a virtuous one. Indeed, perfect sincerity would expose its possessor either to ridicule, to hatred, or to the imputation of insanity. And any general character approaching to real virtue could not exist under the chilling influence of the existing arrangements of society. This we must acknowledge, with however much regret. But we must be careful in regard to the conclusions we deduce from the fact. We must weigh the matter well, before we admit, that human nature is *necessarily* thus corrupt under EVERY system—or utterly abandon the idea, that the most noble and superior sentiments, good faith, sincerity, generosity, independence and fortitude, kind and social, and charitable feelings, are its inherent qualities, which require only the influence of a mild and genial climate, to draw them forth—and adopt in its place the gloomy picture, loaded with disgusting defects, and sordid qualities, which is held up to us as a true representation of our nature, and over which we may brood, till fancy herself either discovers, or creates the resemblance. If it be correct, then may we give up all hope of any great or permanent improvement in this world, for the prospect before us is dismal and bleak, and discouraging indeed. It matters not that the intelligence and beneficence of the Creator is conspicuous alike in the instinct, which directs the smallest insect in the way he should go, and in the principle, which regulates and upholds thousands of worlds in empty space. It matters not that every inferior being seems fitted for the condition assigned to it, for man himself, it seems, is not. In his formation, an all-wise and omnipotent Creator has failed. Man's prospects of happiness are indeed fair and promising, but his heart has been made inherently depraved, and must always remain so—and that mars and blasts them all. To attempt its improvement would be in fact to oppose the fiat of his Creator, which has stamped deceit and depravity even on the earliest consciousness of infancy.

In inculcating that religion teaches such a doctrine, let us at least confess to ourselves, that it is one, whose direct tendency is, *to discourage all attempts to promote the virtue or the happiness of the world;* and to fill our mind with vague and painful adprehensions for the future ; on the ground, that an *all-good* and *all-powerful* Being has formed, or (which is the same thing) has permitted to be formed in the heart of man, a principle, *which must render all such attempts abortive,* and *all such apprehensions but too well founded.*

Yet this doctrine, and many others of a similar tendency, form part of the religious instruction which is at present given, even to the youngest children. The world is at issue in regard to many of these doctrines ; yet they are unhesitatingly presented, in the most uninteresting and dogmatical manner, to the mind of an infant, and *he* is expected to comprehend them. Can we wonder, that such a mode of proceeding should bring religion into disrepute, and that instructions, given with a view to elevate and ennoble the mind, should in their ultimate effects, but leave behind them an idea of a Being, infinitely powerful indeed, but agitated by human passions, any thoughts of whom it is wise to banish from the mind, as only calculated to terrify and distress ;— and an uneasy, undefined feeling of mysterious dread, just sufficient to embitter any moments, into which thoughts of religion may intrude.

We act unwisely in adopting a system of religious instruction which shall, in any one instance, have been found to produce such a result.

At New Lanark, every opportunity is embraced of inculcating those practical moral principles which religion enjoins; and of storing the minds of the children, with the most important and striking natural facts; but the consideration of any abstruse doctrines is, as far as the religious views of the parents will admit, reserved for an age, when the pupils shall be better fitted to judge for themselves, and to weigh, with an accuracy, which it would be folly to expect from a child, the opposing arguments that are employed to support or to attack disputed points. By this means, the real interests of truth *must necessarily be promoted;* for it is evident that an individual, whose judgment has been thus informed, must be much less likely to reject truth, or to receive error, than it is possible for the unprepared mind of an infant to be.

It appears to us, that if an individual be sincere in his religious profession, whatever peculiar tenets he may hold, he must, on mature consideration, approve of the plan, which is now suggested, as the most certain method of *disseminating his particular opinions* over the world. And simply because each individual believes his own opinions to be true, or he would not entertain them.

If it be admitted that a very large majority of the religions of the world are false—and it is certain, that only one *can* be true—then does the admission furnish an additional argument in favour of this mode of instruction. For it is very unlikely that any false religion would endure such a test; and it is certain, that a religion founded on reason and on truth, must be essentially promoted by it, to the exclusion of all others.

We shall not enter into any arguments in support of the doctrines propounded by Calvin; nor shall we question their truth or accuracy: the discussion is irrelevant to our present purpose; but it appears to us evident to a demonstration, that if these doctrines are true we cannot adopt a more effectual method of inducing the whole world to become Calvinists, than that now recommended. If false, the sooner they are exploded the better.

It is a fair question, whether too little interference in so delicate a subject as that of religion, or too great latitude in religious toleration, can ever exist? That an opposite system has excited the most bitter and violent of all animosities, that it has armed the neighbour against his neighbour, the father against his children, has destroyed the peace and harmony of families and of nations, has deluged the world with blood, and, under the sanction of the most sacred name, countenanced atrocities, during the relation of which we seem to listen to the history, not of men, endowed with reason, but of demons, possessed with an infernal spirit of savage madness—these are facts, which every page of our history must establish. Can we be too tenacious in maintaining a principle, the practical influence of which, is to prevent *the possibility* of their recurrence?

This is the principle that has always regulated the religious instruction, in the New Lanark Schools. An endeavour has been made to rescue human nature from the imputations thrown upon it by the conduct of individuals, actuated by intemperate religious zeal—a conduct, which has often seemed to justify the strongest expressions regarding human deceit and human depravity. At New Lanark these imputations find no support: in pursuing the system adopted there, no cause of complaint has arisen against the natural depravity of our nature. On the contrary, experience seems completely to warrant the opinion, that our nature is a delightful compound, capable, no doubt, of being formed to deceit and to wickedness, but *inherently* imbued neither with the one nor the other—that if fear be excluded as a motive to action, a child will never become deceitful, for it will scarcely have a motive to deceive.—That if a child be taught in a rational manner, it will itself become rational, and thus, even on the most selfish principle avoid wickedness—and that our only legitimate cause for surprise is the consideration, that human nature, as it now exists, is neither so deceitful nor so wicked as the present arrangements of society would seem calculated to make it.

We should apologize for this digression, but that we feel the importance of the subject, and the necessity that those who would improve and re-form the rising generation, should not create to themselves imaginary difficulties, where no real difficulties exist; and that we have seen how much evil may be done, when a teacher first takes it for granted, that his pupils are all depraved and irrational beings, and then treats them as such. The very tone and manner, which such an idea produces, destroys confidence, and creates distrust and dislike. When confidence is lost and dislike excited, the case becomes indeed hopeless; and the teacher, whatever be his talents, will meet with real and increasing difficulties, and daily discover fresh cause for distrust and vexation. Unjust suspicion first *creates* its object, and then glories in the penetration which *dis-*

covered it. His pupils must consider that they have no character to lose, and are thus deprived of a great inducement to virtue. They will thwart him in all his measures, and deceive and oppose him on every occasion; because children will not act generously, unless they be treated with generosity.

Before concluding this important subject, it may be necessary to say; that no allusion has been made in this place to a fact which has already been stated; viz. that the scriptures are and have always been statedly read, and the catechism regularly taught there—because this has been done, not as being considered the proper method of conveying religious instruction to the minds of young children, but because the parents were believed to wish it; and any encroachment on perfect liberty of conscience, was regarded as the worst species of tyrannical assumption.

Besides the studies already mentioned, the children are instructed in music and dancing; which are found essentially to contribute towards moral refinement, and improvement. When properly conducted, each of these acquirements becomes a pure and natural source of enjoyment; and it is a well authenticated fact, that the best method of making a people virtuous, is to begin by rendering their situation comfortable and happy.

SINGING.

All the children above five or six years of age are taught singing, sometimes by the ear, sometimes by the notes. They begin by learning the names and sounds of the notes, and by singing the gamut; then proceed to strike the distances, and finally acquire such a knowledge of the elements of the science of music, as they may easily reduce to practice. The musical notes and signs, as well as a variety of musical exercises, are represented on a large scale, on a rolled canvass, similar to that on which we have mentioned, that the botanical specimens are painted. A small selection of simple airs is made, for the school, every three months. The words to these are printed on sheets, one of which is given to each child. Spirited songs, in the bravura style, are found to be much more adapted to children under ten years of age, than more slow and pathetic airs; into the spirit of which they seldom seem to enter, while the former are uniformly their favourite songs, particularly any lively national airs with merry words. Almost all the children show more or less taste for music; although of course this appears in one child spontaneously, while in another it requires considerable cultivation.

The vocal performers in the evening school are sometimes joined by the instrumental band, belonging to the village. This recurs in general once a week.

DANCING

Is taught, as a pleasant, healthful, natural and social exercise, calculated to improve the carriage and deportment, and to raise the spirits, and increase the cheerfulness and hilarity of those engaged in it. The dances are varied. Scotch reels, country dances, and quadrilles are danced in succession; and by some of the older pupils with a simple and unaffected ease and elegance, which we have never seen surpassed in children of their age.

Besides dancing, the children, boys and girls, now and then go through a few military evolutions, as well to give them the habit of marching regularly from place to place, as to improve their carriage and manner of walking. This species of exercise is never continued long at a time; and stiffness and unnecessary restraint are avoided as much as possible; on the principle, already mentioned, and which pervades the whole of the arrangements in these schools, that whatever is likely to prove unpleasant or irksome to the children, and is not necessary for the preservation of good order, or for some other useful purpose, should never be required of them. At the same time, whatever is really necessary to the proper regulation of the school, is uniformly but mildly enforced.

To prevent any confusion or irregularity,

each teacher is furnished with a list of the lessons, which his class is to receive during the week, and these are of course so arranged, that the lessons of the different classes cannot interfere with each other.

The general appearance of the children is to a stranger very striking. The leading character of their countenances is a mixed look of openness, confidence and intelligence, such as is scarcely to be met with among children in their situation. Their animal spirits are always excellent. Their manners and deportment towards their teachers and towards strangers, are fearless and unrestrained, yet neither forward, nor disrespectful. Their general health is so good, that the surgeon attached to the village, who is in the habit of examining the day scholars periodically, states, as the result of an examination, which took place a few weeks since; that, out of 300 children, only three had some slight complaint; and that all the others were in perfect health. The individual literary acquirements of the greater proportion of the older classes, are such as perhaps no body of children of the same age, in any situation, have had an opportunity of attaining. The writer of the present article has had frequent opportunities of examining them individually; and he has no hesitation in saying, that their knowledge on some of the subjects, which have been mentioned, as forming part of their instruction, is superior to his own.

A sufficient degree of friendly emulation is excited amongst them, without any artificial stimulus; but it is an emulation, which induces them to prefer *going forward with their companions*, to *leaving them behind.* Their own improvement is not their only source of enjoyment. That of their companions they appear to witness with pleasure, unmixed with any envious feeling whatever; and to be eager to afford them any assistance they may require. Some of them have voluntarily undertaken, when any of their companions were necessarily absent during some interesting lecture, to give them all the particulars they should be able to recollect of it, as soon as they returned home.

Although there have always been schools at New Lanark, and although the building which is at present employed as a school, has been open for eight years, yet several material parts of the system have been in operation scarcely two years—so that their ultimate effects cannot yet be fully ascertained. As far as these have yet appeared, however, they have been most satisfactory. It has always been found, that those children, who made the greatest proficiency in their various studies and acquirements, proved subsequently, the best, the most industrious and most intelligent assistants, both as work-people and domestics.

There are persons, who will admit the general consistency and excellency of such a system of education, but who will, nevertheless, object to it, as totally unadapted to the lower or working classes.

That true knowledge uniformly conduces to happiness is a fact, which, though it was denied in the dark ages of the world, is very generally admitted at the present day.

The acquisition of true knowledge, there-

fore, must increase the happiness of those
who acquire it. And if the lower classes
have fewer outward sources of enjoyment,
than their more wealthy neighbours, then
does it become the more necessary and just,
that they should be furnished with means of
intellectual gratification.

We admit, that the lower classes cannot
receive such an education, and yet remain
in their present ignorant and degraded state.
We admit, that it will make them intelligent
and excellent characters. That, when they
are placed in a situation which is really improper, it will necessarily make them de-
sirous of changing and improving it. We
admit, that the real distance between the
lowest and the highest ranks will be de-
creased. That the ultimate result will be
such an improvement of habits, dispositions
and general character in those in subordinate
situations, as will induce us to regard them
in the light of assistants rather than of dependants. We admit, that its general introduction will gradually render all ranks much
more liberal, better informed, more accom-
plished, and more virtuous than the inhabi-

tants of Great Britain are at this moment. And that, in short, its direct tendency will be, to enlighten the world, to raise all classes without lowering any one, and to re-form mankind from the least even to the greatest.

But we misconceive its tendency, and mistake its effects, if we imagine that real, solid intellectual improvement, will ever induce the lower classes to envy the situation, or covet the possessions of the wealthy. Or that it will ever raise any of them above a proper employment, or render them dissatisfied with any state of things, that is really beneficial to themselves or useful to society. Or that it will create seditious principles, or excite revolutionary ideas in their minds. Or, in short, if we suppose that true knowledge will ever conduce to misery. We are in error if we conceive, that it is more pleasant to be surrounded by servile dependants, than by enlightened assistants—or, if we believe, that even the selfish interests of the higher ranks can be promoted by increasing the distance, and thus widening the breach between them and another class of their fellow-creatures—or that the sufferings and degradation of the one class can, in any way, increase the actual enjoyment of the other.

Indeed, the idea, that such a notion is deliberately entertained by the higher classes, presupposes in them a want of feeling, inconsistent alike with every superior sentiment, and with their own real or permanent happiness.

APPENDIX.

APPENDIX

APPENDIX.

THE following brief " Introduction to the Arts and Sciences," is presented to the public merely to explain what sort of outline it is here recommended to give to children, before entering into further details. It was drawn up for the New Lanark Schools, and has been communicated to the elder classes. The teachers are directed to illustrate each idea by any anecdote or interesting particular, which may occur to them, or by drawings or models; and to encourage the children, after hearing a short portion of it, to repeat and explain that portion in familiar language. This they are generally able to do with considerable facility.

A manuscript of this " Introduction" has been transcribed by some of the elder scholars, in order at once to impress it on their minds, and to improve their style of hand-writing.

THE EARTH

On which we live, is a very large ball. It is nearly round, in the shape of a globe. The hills and mountains on its surface, even the highest and largest of them, which are six or seven times higher than any mountain in Great Britain, do not prevent the earth's being round, any more than the roughness on the skin of an orange prevents the orange being round; for they are not so large compared to the whole earth, as the small raised parts, which make the orange skin rough compared to the orange. And, therefore, if we were going to represent the earth by a globe as large as an orange, we should not make the mountains so large as these small inequalities on the skin of the orange.

The earth does not seem to us round, but flat, because we can only see a very, very small part of the outside of the earth at once; and a small part of the outside of a large ball is so very like a flat surface, that we cannot easily distinguish it from one. But we know that the earth *is* round, because people, by travelling for two or three years, in the same direction, came at last to the place they set out from. These people travelled round the world.

We do not know whether the earth is solid or not; because we have never seen the inside, except a very short way under the surface.

It is always turning round with us. Yet we do not feel it moving, because every thing we see moves along with us. In the same way, that if a ship sails on a smooth sea, and we are in one of the rooms in the inside of the ship, we cannot tell whether the ship is moving or not; for it does not seem to us to move at all.

The earth is warmed by a much larger globe than itself, called the sun. The sun is a very great way from the earth. If it were too near, every thing would be burnt up. If the sun did not give us heat, nothing could grow or live.

A candle, or any light, can only shine on one half of a globe at a time; the other half is dark. In the same way, the sun can only shine on one half of the earth at once, while the other half, on which it cannot shine, must be dark. This is the reason why it is sometimes day, and sometimes night. The part of the earth we are on, is turned to the sun in the daytime, and turned away from it at night.

You will be told afterwards, why the days are sometimes longer, and sometimes shorter; and why it is hot in summer, and cold in winter.

If you were going to draw a picture of a ball,

you could only draw one half of it at once. Then you would require to turn it round, and draw the other half. That is the reason why the whole earth is drawn on two hemispheres. As you cannot draw it round on paper, it seems flat, but each hemisphere should in fact be a half ball. Every other map, although all maps are drawn flat, represents a part of the outside of the large ball we live on, so that, to be quite correct, it should be raised from the paper.

The world, or any part of the world, can be drawn on a very large map, or on a very small one, in the same way that you can draw the same house on a large piece of paper, and make it large, or on a small piece, and make it small. This is called drawing on a *large scale*, or on a *small scale*.

Part of the outside of the earth is covered with water. The part that is not covered with water is called land, and is not quite half as large as the other.

The whole of the outside of the earth is, therefore, either land or water.

The whole of the earth is surrounded by air.

EVERY thing that is in, or on the earth, is called a *substance*. Each of these substances is supposed to consist of very small particles, much too small to be seen.

All these substances remain on, or in the earth, and the different parts of each of them keep together;—because all substances are drawn towards each other, we do not know how or why.

The larger a substance is, the more it draws another to it; because it has more particles than a smaller body, and each of these particles draws a little. This is the reason why the earth draws every substance to itself; or, in other words, why substances *fall* if we let them; and why they *press* with what is called their *weight*, upon any thing that supports them.

When any body falls, it draws the earth a *very* little upwards, in the same way that the earth draws it downwards. But all bodies are so small compared to the earth, and the earth is so large, compared to them, that we do not see the earth fall to them, or move towards them, and they fall to it.

The different substances on the earth would fall towards each other if they were larger than the earth; but we never see them do so, because none of them are nearly so large as the earth; and, therefore, although they *are* drawn to each other, yet the earth draws them towards itself so much more forcibly, that they are held down to the earth, and cannot fall towards each other.

This is the reason that it requires an effort to raise one of our arms or legs, and that it falls again if we let it.

This is the reason, too, why we never fall off the earth when it is turning round; for (because the earth draws us strongly towards itself,) we always remain standing, or sitting, or lying on it. *We call that which is* IN *the earth,* BELOW *us; and we say, that that which surrounds the earth,* (for instance, the clouds,) *is* ABOVE *us.* *Therefore,* however the earth turns, we always stand or sit with our feet downwards, and our heads upwards; that is, with our feet turned towards the earth, and our heads away from it.

If a larger substance than the earth were to come near the earth, it would draw the earth to it; that is, the earth, and every thing that is upon the earth, would fall to it; but although there *are* many larger substances than the earth, which you will be told about afterwards, they are not near enough to draw the earth to them.

For, the *nearer* substances are to each other, the more strongly they are drawn together. This is the reason why the small particles of every thing or substance remain together, and why it requires force to separate, cut, or divide any thing.

This inclination of substances to fall towards each other, is called *attraction ;* and when they are drawn together, we say they attract each other.

If substances did not attract each other, any power, that could set them, even in the least degree in motion, (for instance, the wind,) would blow every thing to pieces ; and the whole world would be separated into small particles in a very short time.

Whenever the force of the wind on a substance is stronger than the attraction *of the earth* to that substance, then the substance is lifted into the air ; and whenever the attraction becomes stronger than the force of the wind, it falls again.

Whenever the force of the wind on the particles of a substance is stronger than the attraction of these particles *to each other*, then that substance is blown to pieces.

Whenever the attraction of the particles of a body or substance *to the earth* is stronger than their attraction *to each other*, then that body falls to pieces ; that is, each of the separate particles the body is made of falls to the earth, *as soon as the* SIZE *of the earth makes the attraction greater, than the* CLOSE-NESS *of these small particles to each other, makes it.* For the force of the attraction always depends on the *closeness* of the bodies, and on their *size*.

Almost all bodies, which we see, are made of two or more substances, and are then called *compound* bodies. The substances these compound bodies are made of, are called *elements*, or *simple bodies*. We very seldom find simple bodies; that is, we very seldom find bodies made of one substance only.

Although there are so *very* many compound bodies, yet there are very few different kinds of simple bodies, but the different ways in which these bodies come together, make the different objects we see; in the same way that, although there are so few letters in the alphabet, you can make so very many words by putting them together.

We can decompose all compound bodies; that is, we can find out the simple bodies they are made of, but we cannot always put the simple bodies together again, so as to form the compounds we decomposed; for instance, we can decompose flesh or bones, and get the simple substances they are made of; but after we have got these, we cannot make flesh and bones of them again.

———

Every substance belongs to one of three great divisions called Kingdoms, viz.—

The Animal Kingdom;

The Vegetable Kingdom; and

The Mineral Kingdom.

Now, I will tell you how you can generally find out to which kingdom any thing belongs.

ANIMALS change, live, move of themselves, and (most of them, if not all,) think.

VEGETABLES change, live, (cannot move of themselves, and are not supposed to think.)

MINERALS change, (do not live, therefore cannot die or fade, cannot, any more than vegetables, move of themselves, or think.)*

Therefore, animals, vegetables, and minerals, or all substances—change ; animals and vegetables change and live ; animals change, live, move of themselves, and think.

I.—HOW ANIMALS, VEGETABLES, AND MINERALS, CHANGE.

ALL substances are continually changing, either slowly, or quickly ; sometimes increasing ; sometimes decreasing ; sometimes with little or no change that we can perceive ; sometimes by means of an instant and complete change. When animals or vegetables change, so as to increase in size, we say they *grow*.

When an *animal* is born, it is smaller than it will be after it has lived some time. It continues to increase in size, or to grow ; sometimes only for some

---

* These divisions and definitions are given, not because they were considered the most critically correct that could be adopted, but because they were thought to be simple, and easy of application.

hours; sometimes for many years, till it has attained its full size. Still, however, the different particles of the animal continue moving about, and becoming altered; and the whole body and appearance becomes changed, but slowly. Animals grow so slowly that we cannot see them growing; but we see after some time, that they have become larger, and that their appearance has become altered.

Vegetables begin to grow from a seed, or from a root, when this seed or root is put into the earth, or sometimes when it is merely put into water. Some parts of vegetables grow upwards; those are the parts we see; some downwards into the earth, and these are called roots. Vegetables grow in general more quickly than animals, but still they scarcely ever grow so quickly, that we can see them growing.—Most vegetables grow during the hot months of the year; and cease to grow, and even lose part of their growth, in winter. The particles a vegetable is made of, move about in it, and become gradually altered, as well as those of an animal. Some vegetables grow much larger than any animals.

Minerals change, as well as animals and vegetables, but in a very different manner to these, and *very* much slower, often without seeming to change at all. Some of them, however, become many thousand times larger than any animal or vegetable.

The whole body of the earth, as far as we know, is composed of minerals, which have been changing for a very long time.

There are a very great many more mineral substances in the earth than animal or vegetable substances; for animal and vegetable substances grow merely on the surface of the earth, whereas, the earth itself is probably made of mineral substances.

11.—HOW ANIMALS AND VEGETABLES LIVE.

You have just been told, that animals, vegetables, and minerals, are continually changing,—sometimes growing larger, sometimes becoming less; but you know, that animals and vegetables grow quite in a different way from minerals. First of all, they grow quicker; then, animals cannot grow unless they are fed, nor vegetables unless they are planted. Then again, animals and vegetables grow larger for a certain time; then they continue nearly the same size; then they become less and less vigorous, till at last they always change completely, and become what we call *dead*. The animal does not move about then, nor take food, as it used to do; the vegetable does not grow in the warm months, and lose its growth in the cold ones, as it used to do. It falls to the ground; and the roots and branches of the dead vegetable, and the body of the dead animal, gradually fall to pieces, and mix with the minerals and vegetables around them, and change along with them.

Now, this way in which animals and vegetables change till they die, is called *living*; and the sudden change they all undergo, when they no longer continue this mode of existence, is called *death*. Minerals do not grow in this way for a time, and then change suddenly; therefore, minerals do not live or die.

Animals cannot live without eating food, which is either an animal, vegetable, or mineral substance, chiefly a vegetable one; nor without drawing in and breathing out the air with which the earth is surrounded. If they are without food or air, for a short time, almost all animals will die. This food, and this air, must be proper for the animal, or he cannot live either. Some animals eat one kind of food, and some another. Each different species of animals requires different kinds of food to keep it alive. Some kinds of air, too, would kill an animal, if he were to breathe them: these are sometimes found a little below the surface of the earth. But the air which surrounds the earth is, almost everywhere, fit for breathing; only it is better in one place than another.

Part of the food an animal eats, mixes with the

particles of the body of the animal; and the air the animal breathes takes away some of these particles. These particles are thus continually in motion, so as gradually to change the animal. Most animals have blood, which is red in some, and white in others. It moves about in the body of the animal as long as it lives. If a severe blow or stab prevent these things from going on, the animal is killed.

Some animals do not live for one day; others live for about 200 years. We do not know what is the longest time some animals may live.

Vegetables cannot live, any more than animals, without food, nor without air. Their roots receive nourishment from the ground, or from water, and this nourishment is circulated all over the vegetable. The other parts of the vegetable, particularly the leaves, are acted upon by the air which surrounds it, so that circulation is continually going on throughout the vegetable. Some vegetables require one kind of ground, and some another. Some vegetables live only one summer, and these are called *annuals;* some live longer probably than any animals; some are said to have lived about 1000 years.

If a vegetable be cut in two, that part which remains in the ground generally continues to live, and the other part dies.

Some animals and vegetables can only live in warm countries, and some few only in cold ones.

III.—HOW ANIMALS *MOVE* AND *THINK.*

SOME animals move on land, and some in water. Most land animals move about by means of feet, which they put forwards and backwards as they please. A few land animals move without feet, by drawing their bodies together, and then stretching them out again. Some land animals can move about in the air, without touching the land, by means of wings, with which they continue to strike the air, as long as they wish to move about. Water animals move about in the water, by means of fins, which are grisly substances, which they can move at pleasure, so as to answer the purpose of our feet. Only one kind of water animal that we know, can move about in the air, and it can only do so for a short time.

Most animals have five senses; viz. the senses of seeing, hearing, feeling, smelling, tasting. Every thing that surrounds them makes an impression on the senses, perhaps somewhat in the same way that we can make an impression on any thing, for instance by striking or pressing it. If we strike or press any thing it receives the stroke or pressure; and if any thing comes before our eyes, our eyes receive the image or impression of that thing. If they did not, we could not see what it was like;—and the same with the rest of their senses.

We certainly do not know *how* our senses get these impressions, but we know that they *do* get them; for we see things with our eyes, hear with our ears, feel with our fingers and other parts of our bodies, smell with our noses, and taste with our mouths. If we could not see, hear, smell, taste or feel, we could know nothing of what is about us; so that every thing we know, we know by our senses. We could not think at all if we knew nothing, and we always think according to what we know, or according to these impressions. Therefore these impressions give us thoughts, and after we have thought, then we move about or act. So that you see the impressions which we receive by our senses, cause us to move about or act.

Now Vegetables have not these senses. They do not see, hear, feel, smell or taste. Therefore they can neither think, nor move about, nor act.

———

Now I will tell you what are the different kinds of knowledge, which have been obtained by the senses of different men.

All knowledge belongs either to an *art* or a *science*.

Whatever tells us of the nature and properties of any substance, is a *science*.

Whatever teaches us how to produce any thing, is an *art*.

The principal sciences are—

Astronomy, Geography, Mathematics, Zoology, Botany and Mineralogy—Chemistry.

The arts are—

Agriculture, Manufactures, Architecture, Drawing, (including Sculpture,) Music, and a few others of less importance.

Almost all these arts depend upon sciences, for it is necessary to know what are the nature and qualities of substances, before we can produce them.

I am now going to tell you what these sciences tell us about, and what these arts teach us.

ASTRONOMY.

There are, as I told you, many other very large bodies besides the earth, some of them much larger than the earth. These bodies are the sun, the moon and the stars. Astronomy teaches us all that is yet known about them; and about their sizes and distances from one another. They are so far from this earth, that we do not know much about them.

GEOGRAPHY

Is the knowledge of the countries that are on the surface of the earth. It tells us what these different countries are like, and how they are divided. It tells us of the manners and customs of the people who live in them, and what animals, vegetables and minerals are found there.

MATHEMATICS

Teaches us how to number and to measure different bodies, and how to tell their proportionate sizes to each other.

ZOOLOGY

Is the natural history of animals; or the knowledge of the formation, appearance, habits, and dispositions of animals.

As men and women are animals, it tells us about them; for instance, about their bodies, about the blood, flesh, bones, sinews, joints, and all the different parts of the body. It explains to us, as far as can yet be explained, how they live, how they move about, how they feel and think, and how they should be treated; but in all these things there is a great deal that has not yet been discovered, and that we cannot understand.

That part of the natural history of men and women, which tells us what men and women did before we were born and since that time, is called *History.* We are not sure that all histories are quite true; because the people who wrote them might have been mistaken, or might have written that, which they knew did not happen. However, when different writers of history, who did not know one another and had not seen what one another wrote, tell us the same thing, it is more likely to be true, than when only one writer tells us so.

It is more difficult to tell whether what we read in history is true or not, than whether what we read about the earth and its productions is true, because we can see the earth, and what is on it, but we cannot see what happened before we were born; nor if it be long since, even see the persons, who were there when any event happened.

That part of Zoology which tells us about men and women, is the most important science in the world, because you will grow to be men and women, and then you will find how very useful it is to know as much as is yet known about yourselves. Now although every thing you will hear about yourselves does really belong to Zoology, yet there is so much of it, and it is so very different from the natural history of other animals, that it is generally found convenient not to include it under Zoology, but to divide it into a number of different sciences, which you will hear of when you are older and better able to understand them.

BOTANY

Is the knowledge of all substances that belong to the vegetable kingdom, therefore of all trees, shrubs, flowers, fruits, and other vegetable productions.

MINERALOGY

Is the knowledge of the substances of which the earth is made.

That part of Mineralogy, which tells us about the interior (or inside) of the earth, and about large mineral masses, is called *Geology.*

We know very little about Geology, because we have never been able to get more than two miles into the earth. Now it is 8000 miles through the earth, so that we must have gone 4000 times farther than two miles to see what was all through the earth.

Now I will tell you what the arts are, that I mentioned to you.

AGRICULTURE.

The greater part of the food we eat is produced from the ground. Agriculture is the art of producing this food. It is by far the most useful and necessary employment in the world, because we could scarcely live without it.

MANUFACTURES.

Every thing we wear and every thing we use, except food, is produced by manufactures. The greater part of these things is made by machines. One machine often does as much work as a great many men and women. New machines are found out almost every day.

Small manufactures are often called trades; for instance the trade of a shoemaker, tailor, &c.

ARCHITECTURE

Is the art of building the houses in which men and women live. A hut is a very small house which was easily built, and which has only one or two rooms. A palace is a very large house, which contains many rooms, and which costs much trouble in building.

DRAWING

Is the art of representing objects, so that a person who sees the drawing may know what the object is like, although he has never seen the object itself. The more like the drawing seems to the object it is meant to represent, the better it is done. Most drawings are made on paper, canvass or ivory. Drawings of persons are called portraits.

Sculpture is the art of representing objects by cutting wood or stone like them.

MUSIC

Is the art of producing pleasant sounds by means of the voice, or of different instruments. The knowledge of the rules required to compose music is called Thorough Bass.

———————

Most of these sciences might be included under CHEMISTRY; and even many of the arts depend upon it; for Chemistry is, in fact—

The knowledge of the properties of all substances, and of the manner in which all simple substances are combined, and all compound substances decomposed.

Under Chemistry, however, *is generally understood* the knowledge of some of the properties of such of the simple substances as we have already discovered, and of a few of their combinations, as well as the way to make some of these combinations. Even in this contracted signification, Chemistry includes a part of the sciences of Zoology, Botany and Mineralogy. The substances it tells us about at present are chiefly minerals; so that it is the most connected with Mineralogy.

We do not know nearly so much about Chemistry as we may expect to know, when people have paid more attention to it and tried more experiments.

In order to get an easier knowledge of the sciences and arts, we learn to read, write, and to understand languages, the arithmetical signs, and the musical notes and signs. But these are not real knowledge. We only learn them, that we may be able to acquire knowledge by means of them. All real knowledge is not included in any of these, but only in the arts and sciences.

Trade or commerce is the system of arrangements, by which the productions of nature and of the arts are at present distributed.

Any new fact in science is called a *discovery*: any new mode of producing, an *invention*.

No science or art is by any means complete. People are learning something new in all of them almost every day. That is; there are discoveries and inventions made almost every day.

GLASGOW:
ANDREW & JOHN M. DUNCAN,
Printers to the University.